Hidden in the Snow

Barbara Taylor

QEB Publishing

Project Editor: Angela Royston
Designer: Matthew Kelly
Picture Researcher: Maria Joannou

Copyright © QEB Publishing, Inc. 2011

Published in the United States by
QEB Publishing, Inc.
3 Wrigley, Suite A
Irvine, CA 92618

www.qed-publishing.co.uk

Library of Congress Cataloging-in-Publication Data

Taylor, Barbara, 1954-
 Hidden in the snow / Barbara Taylor.
     p. cm. -- (Camouflage)
 Includes index.
 Summary: "Gives examples of how Arctic and Antarctic animals use camouflage to help them adapt to their
habitats and hide from predators"--Provided by publisher.
 ISBN 978-1-60992-080-7 (library bound)
 1. Animals--Adaptation--Polar regions--Juvenile literature. 2. Camouflage (Biology)--Juvenile literature. I. Title.
 QL104.T486 2012
 591.47'2--dc22

                      2011009127

ISBN 978 1 60992 188 0 (saddle stitched)

Printed in China

Picture credits
(t=top, b=bottom, l=left, r=right, fc=front cover, bc=back cover)
Alamy Alaska Stock LLC fc; **Corbis** Andrew Parkinson 15b, Wayne Lynch/All Canada Photos 21b; **FLPA** Michio Hoshino/
Minden Pictures 4, Konrad Wothe/Minden Pictures 5l, Tom Vezo/Minden Pictures 5r, Michael Quinton/Minden Pictures
7t, Jurgen & Christine Sohns 1, 12, Reinhard Hölzl/Imagebroker 13l, Patricio Robles Gil/Minden Pictures 14, Michael
Quinton/Minden Pictures 15t, Franz Christoph Robi/Imagebroker 16, Hiroya Minakuchi/Minden Pictures 17r, Tui De Roy/
Minden Pictures 18, Jim Brandenburg/Minden Pictures 21t; **Nature Picture Library** Chris Gomersall 6, Staffan Widstrand
8, Steven Kazlowski 11, Doug Perrine 17l, Pete Cairns 20; **Photolibrary** Doug Allan 7b, J-L. Klein & M-L. Hubert 9, Peter
Arnold Images 10, AlaskaStock 13r, Peter Arnold Images/Gerard Lacz 19; **Shutterstock** Jan Martin Will bc, Hunter 2/3,
Lizard 22-23, Armin Rose 24.

Front cover: A baby seal hides
on the bumpy ice that covers
the Arctic Ocean.

The words in **bold**
are explained in the
Glossary on page 22.

Contents

Hiding in the Snow 4

As White as Snow 6

Hunting in the Snow 8

Animal Special Great White Bears 10

Hiding from Hunters 12

Babies and Chicks 14

Light and Dark 16

Animal Special Penguin Patterns 18

Changing Color 20

Glossary 22

Index 23

Notes for Parents and Teachers 24

Hiding in the Snow

Animals that live in cold, snowy places are good at hide-and-seek. The animals hide by blending in with their background. This is called **camouflage.**

Some animals are white to match the snowy ground. Baby harp seals have white fur. They are born on the ice and stay there until they grow up.

▲ Baby harp seals keep very still so that polar bears and other hunters will not see them.

Rocky Ground

Other animals, such as gyrfalcons, live in places where rocks show through the snow. They have brown, gray, and white patterns to match the rocks.

▲ A gyrfalcon flies close to the ground. It is looking for prey.

ANIMAL TALK

- Animals that hunt and kill other animals for food are called **predators.**

- The animals that they hunt are called **prey.**

▶ The Arctic wolf has pale fur that matches the white snow.

As White as Snow

The coldest places on Earth are at the tops of high mountains and in the **Arctic** and **Antarctic.**

Many animals have white fur or feathers. A snow petrel's white feathers help hide it from predators such as larger sea birds.

sharp eyes for spotting fish

white feathers ··········>

▲ A snow petrel is about the same size as a pigeon.

Mountain Sheep

Dall sheep live wild on snowy mountains. In winter, the sheep move down the mountains to keep warm. Wolves try to catch them, but the white sheep disappear like ghosts in the snow.

curved horn

▶ Dall sheep live on very steep mountain slopes. Predators find it hard to chase after them.

rough pads on feet for gripping slippery slopes

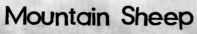

HIDE and SEEK

How many snow petrels can you count in the photo below?

7

Hunting in the Snow

Predators need to get close to their prey to catch a meal. Hunted animals can run very fast, so they may escape before they are caught.

Arctic wolves hunt together in groups, called **packs**. Their white fur blends in with the snow. It is hard for the animals they hunt to spot these white predators.

▶ Arctic wolves can get close to their prey without being seen.

Snow Leopards

Snow leopards have gray fur with dark gray circles. These hunters are almost invisible among the gray mountain rocks.

A snow leopard **stalks** its prey. It slowly creeps closer, keeping as quiet as possible.

ANIMAL TALK

- A pack of wolves can catch an animal much larger than themselves.
- Snow leopards cannot roar. They purr instead.

thick fur for keeping warm

long tail for balancing

9

Great White Bears

Polar bears are the biggest white animals in the world. Polar bears hunt for seals, which usually swim under the ice that covers the sea.

Seals make holes in the ice so they can come up to breathe air. The polar bear waits next to a breathing hole. The bear's white fur camouflages it from the seal.

- A polar bear weighs as much as a small car!

- A polar bear may wait for four hours beside a seal's breathing hole.

▼ A polar bear lies very still as it waits for a seal to pop its head out to breathe.

Surprise Attack

The polar bear pounces on the seal and drags it out of the water. After feeding, the bear cleans its fur by swimming in the water or rolling in the snow.

furry soles on paws for gripping the ice

thick fur and fat for keeping warm

▲ A polar bear rolls in the snow to clean its fur. Polar bears don't feel the cold!

Hiding from Hunters

Hunted animals use camouflage, too. Hiding from a scary predator is one of the best ways to stay alive.

Snowshoe hares often live in groups. If a predator comes near, the hares keep really still. But if the hunter gets too close, the hares scatter. Then the hunter can't decide which hare to follow!

three layers of fur for keeping warm

big furry feet stop the hare sinking into the snow

No Camouflage!

Marmots sleep safely in **burrows** during the snowy winter. They don't need white camouflage!

Musk oxen don't need white camouflage either. Adult musk oxen are so big, with huge **horns**, that no animal attacks them.

long, thick fur

horn

◀ This marmot is looking out for predators.

▶ Adult musk oxen use their big horns to defend their young.

ANIMAL TALK

- Marmots spend eight months a year asleep in their deep burrows.

- Musk oxen stand in a circle around their **calves** to protect them.

13

Babies and Chicks

Baby animals are small and can't defend themselves. But babies are often left alone while their parents find food for them.

Reindeer calves are very small when they are born in summer. Their plain, brown fur blends in well with the brown ground. It helps keep them safe from hunters.

- One-day-old reindeer calves can run faster than a person.

- An eider duck pulls out her fluffy feathers to line her nest and keep her eggs warm.

▲ Baby reindeer have long legs so that they can keep up with the rest of the herd.

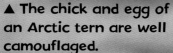
▲ The chick and egg of an Arctic tern are well camouflaged.

Mothers and Chicks

Few trees grow in very cold places, so most birds make their nests on the ground. Female birds usually sit on the nest to keep the eggs warm. These birds need to be well camouflaged.

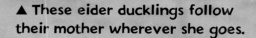
▲ These eider ducklings follow their mother wherever she goes.

Light and Dark

Many animals that live in cold oceans have light tummies and dark backs.

Puffins dive underwater to catch fish. When a fish looks up, it cannot easily see the puffin. The puffin's white belly blends in with the light sky.

When a predator flies above a puffin, the black back of the puffin is hard to see against the dark water.

white belly and breast

◄ Puffins can swim underwater as well as fly in the air.

webbed feet for swimming

blowhole for
breathing

Orcas

The light and dark patterns of
an orca hide it against patches
of light and dark in the
ocean. When it is seen
from the side, the orca
disappears against this
background.

ANIMAL TALK

- Puffins are sometimes called sea parrots because of their colorful bills.

- An orca is a type of dolphin.

▼ Orcas live and hunt in groups called pods.

flippers for
steering

wide tail for
swimming

Penguin Patterns

Penguins have a black back and a white tummy. These colors help camouflage the penguin when it swims in the ocean.

From above, the penguin's black back blends with the dark water. From below, its white tummy blends in with the lighter surface of the ocean.

▲ Camouflage helps the penguin catch food and escape from hunters.

Keeping Warm

Black things soak up heat better than white things do. The penguin's black back soaks up the heat of the sun. This helps the penguin warm up after being in the icy water.

strong beak

smooth top feathers push away the water

fluffy tummy feathers for keeping warm

▲ Different types of penguin have different colors and patterns.

PENGUIN FACTS

- Penguins and polar bears never meet! Penguins live in the Antarctic and polar bears live in the Arctic.

- Penguins cannot fly. They use their wings as flippers when they swim.

Changing Color

Some animals have white fur in winter. Then it changes to brown fur in summer! The fur changes to match the color of the ground.

In winter, snow covers the ground. The Arctic fox's white fur is hard to see against the snow. Its furry coat is very thick and keeps the fox warm.

◄ White fur helps an Arctic fox to get close to its prey.

Summertime

In summer, the snow melts and the ground is covered with rocks. The Arctic fox's fur changes from white to brown to match the rocks.

To change color, furry animals lose their old fur and grow new fur in its place.

HIDE AND SEEK

The Arctic fox hunts Arctic hares. How many Arctic hares can you spot in the photo above?

big ears for hearing prey under the ground

◀ This fox has some of its white winter fur and some of its brown summer fur.

Glossary

Antarctic The frozen continent around the South Pole.

Arctic The frozen ocean and very cold lands around the North Pole.

burrow A long tunnel under the ground. Animals such as marmots dig burrows.

calf The young of many different animals, such as reindeer, whales, and seals.

camouflage Colors, patterns, or markings that help an animal hide by matching its background.

horn A hard growth on the head of a hoofed animal. Horns are often pointed or curved.

pack A group of hunting animals, such as wolves.

predator An animal that hunts and kills other animals for food.

prey An animal that is hunted and killed by a predator.

stalk To creep up slowly and silently. Hunting animals, such as wolves, stalk their prey-

Did you spot them all?
How many animals did you count in the Hide-and-Seek photos? Did you spot four snow petrels on page 7 and eight Arctic hares on page 21? The better the animals are camouflaged, the harder they are to spot!

Index

Antarctic 6, 19, 22
Arctic 6, 19, 22
Arctic fox 20, 21
Arctic hare 21
Arctic tern 15
Arctic wolf 5, 8

baby animals 4, 13, 14–15
birds 5, 6, 14, 15, 16, 17,
    18–19

calves 13, 14, 22
color changes 20–21

dall sheep 7

eider duck 14, 15

feathers 6, 14, 19
fur 4, 5, 6, 9, 10, 11, 12,
    13, 14, 20, 21

gyrfalcon 5

harp seal 4

marmot 13
musk ox 13

orca 17

packs 8, 9, 22
penguins 18–19
pods 17, 22
polar bear 4, 10–11, 19
puffin 16, 17

reindeer 14

seals 4, 10, 11
skua 6, 22
snow leopard 9
snow petrel 6, 7
snowshoe hare 12
stalk 9, 22

wolves 5, 7, 8, 9, 13, 14

Notes for Parents and Teachers

As you share this book with children, ask questions to encourage them to look closely at the detail in the photographs.

What is Snow?
- Explain to the children what snow is. Snow is made up of delicate crystals of ice, with air between them. Light reflected from these crystals makes the snow sparkle and look white.
- Help the children make paper snowflakes and explore symmetry.
- Talk about the feel of snow—its fluffy texture, its lightness, and its coldness—and how it melts and freezes into ice when pressed together in a snowball. Have the children ever made a snowman or a snow hare?

Moving Around
- Camouflage works best when animals keep still, but they have to move sometimes!
- Ask the children to play camouflage hide-and-seek. Each child can pick a surface or area they want to blend into and then dress up to match it, for example a white bedsheet in front of a white wall. After the game is finished, the children can vote for their favorite costume and discuss who was the best camouflaged.

Hunters and Hunted
- Look through the book and ask the children to find the predators (hunters) and the prey (hunted animals). This can be different from one page to the next, as many predators are prey for larger animals! Make a collage of a food chain. Show, for example, an Arctic wolf hunting an Arctic fox, and an Arctic fox hunting an Arctic hare, which eats plants.

Keeping Warm
- Explain how several layers of fur or feathers trap pockets of air. These retain an animal's body heat.
- Because people don't have thick fur like animals, we need to wear warm clothing in the winter. Ask the children how they stay warm when it's cold outside.

Changing Color
- Tell the children that fur and feathers are dead structures, so mammals and birds can't change their color straight away.
- Animals that change color with the seasons grow a whole new coat of fur or feathers. This is called molting. Can the children remember which animals change color?